I0087425

A CourseGuide for

Creation
Care

Douglas J. Moo and
Jonathan A. Moo

Jonathan Lunde, General Editor

ZONDERVAN
ACADEMIC

CONTENTS

Introduction

Welcome to *A CourseGuide for Creation Care*. These guides were
created for formal and informal students alike who want to engage
deeper in biblical, theological, or ministry studies. We hope this
guide will provide an opportunity for you to grow not only in your
understanding, but also in your faith.

How to Use This Guide

This guide is meant to be used in conjunction with the book *Creation
Care* and its corresponding videos, *Creation Care Video Lectures*. After
you have read each chapter in the book and watched the accompanying video lesson, the materials in this guide will help you review and
assess what you have learned. Application-oriented questions are
included as well.

Each CourseGuide has been individually designed to best equip you
in your studies, but in general, you can expect the following components. Most CourseGuides begin every chapter with a "You Should
Know" section, which highlights key terminology, people, and facts
to remember. This section serves as a helpful summary for directing
your studies. Reflection questions, typically two to three per chapter,
prompt you to summarize key points you've learned. Discussion questions invite you to an even deeper level of engagement. Finally, most
chapters will end with a short quiz to test your retention. You can find
the answer key to each quiz at the bottom of the page following it.

For Further Study

CourseGuides accompany books and videos from some of the world's
top biblical and theological scholars. They may be used independently,

or in small groups or classrooms, offering quality instruction to equip students for academic and ministry pursuits. If you would like to engage in further study with Zondervan's CourseGuides, the full lineup may be viewed online. After completing your studies with *A CourseGuide for Creation Care*, we recommend moving on to *A CourseGuide for Cultural Apologetics* and *A CourseGuide for The Color of Compromise*.

CHAPTER 1

What Do Christians Have to Do with Creation?

You Should Know

- Creation care: our ethical responsibilities for the non-human world

- Creation care refers to two interrelated things at the same time: both our ethical obligation and the fundamental basis for that obligation.

- The overarching question in creation care is what role does the non-human creation play in God's plan?

- Environmentalism tends to be *anthropo*-centric.

- The word "nature" is notoriously ambiguous; we use it for all kinds of different meanings, and there are all sorts of possible misunderstandings.

- When it comes to creation care, the gospel imperative to "love our neighbors" must include doing what we can to enable this world to sustain the flourishing of our fellow human beings.

- Christians should be involved in creation care because of the need to address current challenges facing creation, the need to serve as witnesses to God's kingdom in our time, and Scripture's emphasis on our calling as "keepers" of God's creation.

- The factors that explain the sudden outpouring of interest in the environment are the result of unprecedented scientific tools and techniques, as well as the unprecedented speed in development of human technologies.

Reflection Questions

1. Do you agree that "the first and vital step in learning to care for creation is to celebrate creation"? What does the term "creation care" bring to your mind?

2. Why do we use the phrase "creation care"? Why isn't it "nature care"? What's wrong with the word "nature"?

3. Describe the three reasons it's important to talk about creation care.

Discussion Question

1. How do the gospel imperatives to "love our neighbors" and to "love the Lord our God" inform our understanding of creation care? Explain.

Quiz

1. What is the first and vital step in learning to care for creation?
    a) Celebrate creation
    b) Cultivate creation
    c) Utilize creation
    d) Engage creation

2. With appreciation of creation must come _____.
    a) Empathy of creation
    b) Understanding of creation
    c) Celebration of creation
    d) Utilization of creation

3. Which apostle would remind us that right understanding and even acceptance of truth is never enough on its own?
    a) James
    b) Paul
    c) Peter
    d) John

4. Who famously said, "When we try to pick out anything by itself, we find it hitched to everything else in the Universe"?

   a) Ralph Waldo Emerson
   b) Gifford Pinchot
   c) John Muir
   d) Henry David Thoreau

5. (T/F) Concern about the created world as the environment for humans is unnecessary.

6. The demand to put God above all else is one reason we choose to refer to the world as what?

   a) Creation
   b) Environment
   c) Nature
   d) Cosmos

7. (T/F) Using the term "creation care" appropriately privileges *anthropo*-logy over *theo*-logy.

8. Which is NOT one of the reasons Christians should be involved in "creation care"? (p. 26–7)

   a) The need to anchor our creational obligations in humanism
   b) The need to address current challenges facing creation
   c) The need to serve as a witness to God's kingdom in our time
   d) Scripture's emphasis of our vocation as "keepers" of God's creation

9. Which is one of the factors explaining the outpouring of interest in the environment?

   a) People growing increasingly conscientious
   b) Religious oracles calling for the end of the world
   c) The unprecedented speed in development of human technologies
   d) The development of space programs

10. Which is the most important reason to turn our attention to what Scripture says about creation and our role in it?
   a) The unprecedented speed in development of human technologies
   b) The need to address current challenges facing creation
   c) The need to serve as a witness to God's kingdom in our time
   d) Because it is part of God's revelation to us in Scripture

CHAPTER 2

How Do We Think Biblically and Theologically about Creation?

You Should Know

- The strategy of resistance explicitly subordinates the voice of Scripture to another voice.

- A strategy of recovery identifies a core of eco-friendly biblical teaching that is genuinely in the text but has been ignored or muted by cultural assumptions or preoccupation with other issues.

- Building a bridge that carries us from the world of the text to that of the contemporary church requires that our biblical theology be descriptive, prescriptive, inclusive, and canonical.

- The roundabout: the highway leading from text to application with traffic from several secondary roads

- There are three general kinds of traffic that will affect our biblical theology of creation care: historical and systematic theology, culture, and science.

- Historical and systematic theology: Informed by biblical theology, this discipline refers to philosophy and history to provide dogmatic conclusions that instruct the contemporary church.

- The deceptively "objective" task of biblical theology is not as simple as we might sometimes think because we operate at one level removed from the text itself; biblical theologians must make decisions and adopt categories that are not clearly in the text itself.

- Postmodernism: a contemporary philosophy that says no one comes to the biblical text with a blank slate

Reflection Questions

1. Briefly explain the "strategy of resistance," the "strategy of recovery," and the "strategy of revision." Who champions these strategies and why?

2. Describe the approach of Douglas Moo and Jonathan Moo for how to use the Bible to address creation care. Why is it more specific than just "biblical theology"?

3. What are the limitations of the bridge metaphor for biblical theology? What metaphor more accurately describes the "traffic pattern" of biblical theology?

Discussion Question

1. The biblical-theological approach to creation in Scripture requires that we build our bridge out of four materials. Describe those materials.

Quiz

1. What has led many to jettison traditional religions in favor of ones that are seemingly oriented to the earth and nature?
    a) Concerns about epistemology
    b) Extreme skepticism
    c) Concerns about the environment
    d) Scientism

2. (T/F) The book *Greening Paul* surveys different ways Christians might use Scripture to address concerns about creation.

3. Horrell, Hunt, and Southgate identify which two main options for how Paul's letters help us think about creation?

   a) "Resist" the text and assume a "strategy of recovery"
   b) Assume a "strategy of recovery" and "prove" the text
   c) "Prove" the text and "resist" the text
   d) Assume a "strategy of spiritualism" and a "strategy of revision"

4. (T/F) The strategy of resistance explicitly subordinates the voice of Scripture to another voice.

5. Which hermeneutical strategy for reading Paul's letters do Horrell, Hunt, and Southgate opt for?

   a) Recovery
   b) Resistant
   c) Recapitulative
   d) Revisionist

6. When we begin talking about making new meanings in the Bible, we risk dispensing with the authority of _____.

   a) Scripture
   b) The reader
   c) The human author
   d) The context

7. Biblical theology is known as a _____ activity.

   a) First-level
   b) Second-level
   c) Third-level
   d) Fourth-level

8. Which is *not* one of the adjectives used to describe the four materials necessary for building a biblical-theological "bridge"?

   a) Descriptive
   b) Inclusive
   c) Exclusive
   d) Canonical

9. (T/F) The best metaphor for how biblical theology works in our reading of Scripture is a one-way bridge.

10. (T/F) Our culture can enhance our biblical theology by helping us set priorities in our work.

CHAPTER 3

A Beautiful World

You Should Know

- *Bara*: a word only ever used for the activity of God

- Wrong thinking about God can usually be traced back to confusion about the Creator/creation distinction.

- The Babylonian *Enūma Eliš* contains a creation account that is chaotic. Whereas, Genesis contains a creation account that is orderly.

- Genesis 1:16 refers to the sun and moon as the "greater light" and the "lesser light" respectively because the sun and moon were considered deities by other ancient Near Eastern cultures, and use of their names in a creation account could imply validation of their divinity.

- The *telos*, or purpose, of creation is to the glory of God and Christ.

- The contingency of creation—the fact that the world is not necessary and could have been otherwise—means that creation can only be known by actually looking at it, exploring it, and studying it.

- The characteristics of the seven-day account in Genesis 1 include: culminates in God's rest on the seventh day; God creates, separates, and fills previously formless spaces; the world is not portrayed as necessary to God, accidental, or a by-product of something else; Creator/creation distinction implied in verse 16.

- The seven days of creation in Genesis: light, day and night; waters above (sky) and waters below; land separated from sea, vegetation; sun, moon, stars; birds and sea creatures; land animals; God's rest

- Psalm 104 begins and ends with a call to praise God: its first half echoes the creation account in Genesis 1; God is active in creating and sustaining the world; and God's concern with and delight in creation

Reflection Questions

1. List the differences between *Enūma Eliš* and the creation account in Genesis. Do you think the Genesis account is chaotic? Explain your answer.

2. Other than in Psalm 104, where else does Scripture describe the theme of God's glory revealed through his creation?

3. Why is the unique responsibility that human beings have for creation not the same as ownership?

Discussion Question

1. List the limitations of natural theology. Does it have any place in our apologetics? Describe the two New Testament instances where preaching is directed toward people who apparently have no knowledge of the Old Testament.

Quiz

1. Which Babylonian work contains the account of Marduk slaying the chaos monster Tiamat?

    a) The *Aluzinnu*
    b) The Epic of Gilgamesh
    c) Šumma izbu
    d) *Enūma Eliš*

2. (T/F) In Genesis the world was created out of chaos.

3. Where in the Bible does Moses warn the Israelites against the worship of the sun, moon, and stars?

    a) Deuteronomy 17:3

    b) 2 Kings 23:5

    c) Deuteronomy 4:19

    d) Job 31:26–28

4. (T/F) Genesis 1 implies that we need something like empirical science if we are to know God's creation.

5. Which number is symbolic of completeness?

    a) 7

    b) 6

    c) 5

    d) 3

    e) 1

6. (T/F) In Genesis 1, all animals are described as being or having *nephesh khayah*.

7. Which creatures were told, along with humanity, to "be fruitful and increase in number"?

    a) Land beasts and birds

    b) Sea creatures and land beasts

    c) Birds and sea creatures

    d) Creatures that move along the ground

8. Which psalm rings out the loudest and clearest in its praise of God for the richness and diversity of his world?

    a) 104

    b) 97

    c) 102

    d) 19

    e) All of the above

9. (T/F) The fullness of who God is and the particularity of his revelation of himself in his Word cannot be learned through natural theology.

10. Which term describes the blessings of God's provision in creation and the experience of joy that finds its source only in him?

a) Prevenient grace
b) Common grace
c) Natural grace
d) Special grace

CHAPTER 4

Members, Rulers, and Keepers of Creation

You Should Know

- Humankind's possession of a "soul" does not distinguish it from other living things, all of whom are also animated by God's same life-giving Spirit.

- The prophets and the psalmists regularly remind us regarding our place in God's creation, that we are not as special as we may think.

- Psalm 8:5: "You have made them a little lower than the angels and crowned them with glory and honor."

- The image of God: refers to mankind's relationships with God, each other, and the rest of creation for the purpose of ruling as God's royal representatives

- The dominion mandate: "Be fruitful and increase in number; fill the earth and subdue it"; this command is found in Genesis 1:26–28.

- Genesis 9:6: "Whoever sheds human blood, by humans shall their blood be shed; for in the image of God has God made mankind." This verse addresses the function of the image of God in distinguishing human beings from other creatures; all human beings are created in the image of God and are to be treated as such.

- Characteristics of the "image of God": humans rule the earth as God's royal representatives; reflects the unifying love at the center of the triune God; humans do not bear God's image by virtue of their own merit; all human beings bear God's image (democratization)

- In the context of Genesis 1, the charge to "subdue" the earth suggests the active work of bringing the earth under the appropriate rule of those who bear God's image.

- *Abad*: "to work"; "to serve"

- *Shamar*: "to keep"

Reflection Questions

1. Summarize the various passages where the Bible reminds us of our relative insignificance within the wider community of creation.

2. What is the purpose of God's creation of humanity in his image? Summarize the meaning of the Hebrew word for "subdue" (*kabash*). What does the charge to "subdue" the earth mean in the context of Genesis 1? Summarize the meanings of the words *abad* and *shamar* within the context of Genesis 2:15. How does this impact our human vocation?

3. How is God's value of all of life seen in the Noahic covenant? Why would God's commitment in this covenant to preserve his creation be particularly important to early readers of Genesis? What similarity does this covenant bear with the Abrahamic covenant?

Discussion Question

1. Drawing on what you have learned so far, elaborate on the importance of caring for the earth as an inescapable part of who God has created us to be.

Quiz

1. Where does the apostle Paul exhort us to offer our bodies as "living sacrifices" to God?
    a) 1 Corinthians 15
    b) Ephesians 4
    c) Romans 12
    d) Galatians 3

2. (T/F) Human possession of the life-giving breath of God distinguishes us from other living things.

3. Aside from Genesis 1:26–28, where else does the Old Testament make explicit reference to mankind being created in the "image of God"?

    a) Genesis 5

    b) Genesis 9

    c) Genesis 3

    d) Genesis 2

4. (T/F) The image of God means being placed into a particular set of relationships for the purpose of ruling as owners of God's creation.

5. The stress in Scripture on the universality of the image of God demands that we do which of the following?

    a) Recognize that all of God's creatures have a "living soul"

    b) Recognize that all of creation belongs to God

    c) Recognize that we are called to take dominion over God's creation

    d) Recognize the image of God in all human beings

6. (T/F) Humans are not the only creatures who have been given the mandate to "fill" space.

7. A biblical understanding of kingship makes impossible any interpretation of *dominion* in Genesis 1:26–28 as what?

    a) Domination

    b) Stewardship

    c) Regency

    d) Supervision

8. Which theme(s) from the story of Noah is/are of particular importance for our understanding of the relationship between humanity, God, and creation?

    a) God's use of the righteous Noah to save other creatures

    b) The covenant God establishes with all of creation

    c) God's decision to judge human evil by destroying the earth

    d) Noah's sacrifice offering up a "pleasing aroma" to the LORD

e) Both A & B

f) Both A & C

9. (T/F) Noah's ark reminds us that our role of working and taking care of the earth includes the good use and application of technology.

10. Which of Jesus's parables illuminates something of the nature of our responsibilities within creation?

a) The vinedresser

b) The sower

c) The wise steward

d) The talents

CHAPTER 5

Humanity and the Earth, Israel and the Land

You Should Know

- What has always been required of us is responsible care for and attention to our own locality.

- The heavens and the earth are called upon to witness the covenant between God and his people whom he is establishing in the land.

- The only way that Israel and the land itself will be sustained and find life and blessing is in fidelity to God, practicing restraint, cultivating the land, and taking ownership over the land.

- The shedding of the blood of animals for the people's sins implies an intimate connection between human life and the life of other creatures.

- Sustainability: people using resources in a way that is healthy for both people and land

- The restrictions in Israel's law code about not mixing creatures or sowing two seeds together reflect a cautiousness about not intruding on the divine.

- The parable of the rich fool: an example of failure to remember God as the source and goal of all things

- Characteristics of the Sabbath and the Jubilee: intended for foreigners residing in Israel; intended for Israel's animals; every seventh year there is no sowing, pruning, or reaping; every forty-nine years there is liberty for indentured servants and redistribution of the land

Reflection Questions

1. The health of the land and its ability to sustain human life are dependent on what? What part of the Bible will the Hebrew prophets turn to again and again to challenge God's people and to interpret their experiences in the land?

2. Sustainable living means adopting practices that preserve or enhance the ability of people and all of life to thrive now and into the future. Give two examples of this principle at work in the Bible.

3. Explain the principles behind the Sabbath and Jubilee years. Where can the seriousness with which the biblical writers treat Sabbath rest be inferred? How does the Chronicler interpret the exile?

Discussion Question

1. What are the similarities and differences between the vocation of Israelites on the land in the Old Testament and the vocation of Christians on earth today?

Quiz

1. In which book does the Bible hint that Canaan is a land distinct from others and will require practices particularly suited to its conditions?

    a) Deuteronomy
    b) Exodus
    c) Genesis
    d) Leviticus

2. (T/F) The land of Canaan is called upon to witness the covenant between God and his people whom he is establishing in the land.

3. A biblical ecological vision includes an understanding of which of the following?

    a) Good tilling
    b) Good cultivating

    c) Good preserving

    d) Good work

4. (T/F) The health of the land and its ability to sustain human life are moreover dependent on environmental concerns.

5. The Hebrew prophets turned again and again to _____ to challenge God's people and to interpret their experiences of drought, ruin, and conquest.

    a) The Psalter

    b) The historical narratives

    c) Covenant language

    d) Oracles

6. (T/F) Israel's law reveals that the land and its creatures are considered morally insignificant.

7. Which New Testament book states, "It is impossible for the blood of bulls and goats to take away sins"?

    a) Hebrews

    b) 1 Peter

    c) 1 Corinthians

    d) Ephesians

8. The importance of _____ even in the context of overflowing abundance is one that Israel had already learned from its time in the wilderness.

    a) Scarcity

    b) Disparity

    c) Restraint

    d) Forwardness

9. The observance of Sabbath and _____ years for the land itself serves to remind Israel that God is the true owner and sustainer of the earth.

    a) Festival

    b) Jubilee

26 | Creation Care

c) Harvest
d) Sacrificial

10. (T/F) The Chronicler interprets Israel's exile as a time when the land finally enjoys its Sabbath rest.

CHAPTER 6

A Creation Subject to Frustration

You Should Know

- Basil of Caesarea: Cappadocian father who said, "Not a single thing has been created without a reason."

- The Fall narrative implies that had Adam and Eve lived in obedience to God, they then would have been able to take and eat from the tree of life.

- A reading of Genesis 8:21 implying that the curse was a one-time event that no longer applies in the context of God's cosmic covenant with the postdiluvian world is not tenable because it is in the same context that we learn of the fear that animals will have of human beings.

- The curse on the land seems predominantly or exclusively to be directed at the relationship between human beings and the land.

- The experience of biblical Israel proved to be a recapitulation of the "fall" of Adam and Eve.

- Jeremiah 4 and Isaiah 24 universalize Israel's experience on the land and apply it to the experience of all of creation.

- Romans 8:19–23 highlights the inclusion of all of creation in the hope of the gospel.

- Appropriate responses to the ruin of the earth: lament over human sin and injustice; mourn over the suffering of all of creation; repent and cry out to God for mercy; take our responsibilities in and for creation seriously

Reflection Questions

1. The relationship between humankind and the earth is fraught, and the end, the *telos*, for which God created all things can no longer be reached (unless God changes the situation). Where is this thwarting of God's purposes seen most clearly? Discuss how Adam and Eve's actions frustrated possibilities.

2. What is the problem in Isaiah 24:5? What does the term "everlasting covenant" refer to? Describe how Jeremiah 4 and Isaiah 24 universalize Israel's experience on the land and apply it to the experience of all of creation.

3. Summarize Romans 8:19–23. Why is this an especially important text for creation care?

Discussion Question

1. If we acknowledge that creation will continue to suffer brokenness until the return of Christ, what is our goal in caring for creation now? What does that look like in your life?

Quiz

1. Which Cappadocian father said, "Each of the things that have been made fulfills its own particular purpose in creation"?
   a) Basil of Caesarea
   b) Gregory of Nyssa
   c) Gregory of Nazianzus
   d) Eustathius of Sebaste

2. (T/F) The lesson of Genesis, Job, and Psalms is that all of God's vast and wild creation are valuable parts of the goodness of the whole.

3. (T/F) The thwarting of God's purpose is seen most clearly when Cain murdered Abel and was himself cursed from the ground.

CHAPTER 16

Hebrews

Jesus as Priest

You Should Know

- The author of Hebrews portrays Jesus Christ distinctively as a priest who, having offered none other than himself as the completely sufficient sacrifice for sins, now ministers in the heavenly sanctuary.

- Hebrews emphasizes the superiority of Christ over every aspect and hero of Old Testament religion ensuring that the recipients of the letter do not apostatize from Christianity back to Judaism.

- The authorship of Hebrews has nearly always been unknown, though much of church history has leaned toward Paul.

- It is possible, though tenuous, that Hebrews was written before Nero's persecution in the late 60s.

- Hebrews makes significant use of OT quotations and allusions and emphasizes Christ's superiority in every aspect over every hero of OT religion.

- Hebrews was probably written to a Hellenistic Jewish-Christian audience most likely in Rome.

- Hebrews seeks to encourage perseverance and warn against apostasy in the face of persecution.

- Christ's superiority over: the prophets, the angels, Moses, Joshua, and Aaron

- Apostasy: renouncing Christ willfully and utterly

- Melchizedek: a priest of God who means "king of righteousness"; so also is Christ

Reflection Questions

1. Who are three possible authors of Hebrews and why? Who are the addressees of Hebrews and why?

2. Discuss Hebrews' Christology and how perfection and majesty are paralleled with vulnerability in Jesus's priesthood. What does this mean for ministry?

3. How would the author of Hebrews respond to the modern charge that salvation by sacrificial blood is a primitive religious concept?

Essay Question

1. What rhetorical or exegetical forms does the author of Hebrews use in this letter to make his points about Christ?

Quiz

1. The Greek style in Hebrews suggests authorship by _____.
   a) James
   b) Apollos
   c) Clement
   d) Silvanus

2. (T/F) Against authorship of Hebrews by Luke is the Jewish outlook of Hebrews and the Gentile outlook of Luke-Acts.

3. As to the authorship of Hebrews, the early church was:
   a) United on authorship by Paul
   b) Divided over authorship by Paul
   c) United on authorship by Apollos
   d) Divided over authorship by Apollos

4. The restoration of the _____ can come only in the context of a renewed humanity.

   a) Garden of Eden

   b) Cosmos

   c) Tree of life

   d) Ground

5. The experience of _____ proves to be a recapitulation of the "fall" of Adam and Eve.

   a) Biblical Israel

   b) Cain

   c) The flood

   d) The tower of Babel

6. (T/F) In the Hebrew prophets, the earth, and all of its life, is portrayed as suffering as a consequence of the people's sin.

7. Paul's description of creation as "groaning" picks up the language of _____ used in the Old Testament to describe the plight of the earth when subject to human evil and injustice, by experiencing drought and ruin.

   a) Mirth

   b) Weal

   c) Judgment

   d) Mourning

8. (T/F) The only answer for how God subjected creation to futility is that he subjected it to Adam and to all of humankind.

9. Scripture says that creation's suffering is the direct result of which thing(s)?

   a) Its own fault

   b) Human sin

   c) Satan's intervention

   d) God's judgment

   e) All of the above

   f) Both B & C

   g) Both B & D

10. Which biblical passage contains the verse, "Return to the Lord your God, for he is gracious and compassionate, slow to anger and abounding in love, and he relents from sending calamity"?

   a) Romans 8:26–27
   b) Jeremiah 14:13–14
   c) Joel 2:12–13
   d) 1 Corinthians 15:42, 50
   e) All of the above

CHAPTER 7

Jesus and Creation

You Should Know

- There is no more dramatic demonstration of the goodness of creation than the incarnation.

- John 1:3 says that through Jesus "all things were made; without him nothing was made that has been made."

- Jesus Christ is included in the identity of the one God. Through him all things were made. He sustains the world. He became a part of his own creation.

- The incarnation rules out for Christians any philosophy that would deny the reality or goodness of the physical world, because if God himself can take on the stuff of this earth, then the material stuff of this earth cannot be evil.

- God could become incarnate in any creature other than a human being because of the inextricable connectedness of all of God's good creation and because there is no *a priori* reason to the contrary.

- Jesus as the Last Adam: This is necessary for Christ to reconcile us to God.

- Jesus's temptation in the wilderness: Jesus passed the test, unlike Adam and Eve in Eden and Israel in her wilderness wanderings.

- The temptations Satan posed when Jesus was in the wilderness: turn stones into bread, take advantage of divine protection, and choose the easy way of inheriting the world's kingdoms

- Jesus's restoration of the relationship between humanity and creation is evident in Mark's use of the phrase "with the wild animals."

Reflection Questions

1. Why is there no more dramatic a demonstration of the goodness of creation than the incarnation?

2. What is central to the meaning of the "kingdom of God" proclaimed by Jesus? What does Matthew call this "kingdom" and what's the significance of this moniker? What will happen if we attend to what Jesus actually has to say about the transformed life in the here and now?

3. How does Jesus's resurrection and the promise of new creation in him inform our understanding of creation's goal, or *telos*?

Discussion Question

1. How does what we learn from Jesus about what it is to be truly human apply to the practice of creation care? Why does creation benefit from the redemption brought about by Jesus?

Quiz

1. There is no more dramatic demonstration of the goodness of creation than the _____.

    a) Ascension
    b) Crucifixion
    c) Incarnation
    d) Resurrection

2. Which verse says that Jesus's humanity is like us "in every way"?

    a) Hebrews 2:17
    b) Philippians 2:7
    c) 1 Timothy 6:16
    d) Colossians 1:16

3. (T/F) It is necessary that Christ be a human being so he can be the "Last Adam."

4. Which event in Jesus's ministry particularly evidences his identity as both the new Adam and new Israel?

- a) His turning the water into wine
- b) His raising Lazarus from the dead
- c) His feeding the 5,000
- d) His temptation in the wilderness

5. Which gospel account records that Jesus was "with the wild animals"?

- a) Matthew
- b) Mark
- c) Luke
- d) John

6. (T/F) Jesus being "with the wild animals" in the wilderness is significant because the enmity and brokenness that otherwise marks our relationship with non-human creation is being done away with.

7. Which book in the Bible suggests that when we seek to become like God, we forget our dependence upon each other, the earth itself, and our Creator God?

- a) Hebrews
- b) Romans
- c) Deuteronomy
- d) Genesis

8. Which is NOT one of the signs of the kingdom's presence?

- a) Victory over enemies
- b) Healing of the sick
- c) Physical restoration
- d) Raising to life

9. Which verse says that Jesus "made himself nothing"?

- a) Hebrews 2:17
- b) Philippians 2:7
- c) 1 Timothy 6:16
- d) Colossians 1:16

10. In which gospel does Jesus say that he has come so that his people "may have life, and have it to the full"?

   a) Luke
   b) Matthew
   c) Mark
   d) John

CHAPTER 8

"What Counts Is the New Creation"

You Should Know

- Jesus's death and resurrection: the climax of the redemption story

- Many promises God made to his people concerning the last days have "already" been fulfilled, while many others have "not yet" come to pass and others are fulfilled partially now but await complete fulfillment in the future.

- The land promise is a component of God's promise to Abraham, has a prominent role in God's redemptive plan, was given to Israel, and is universalized in the New Testament.

- The key points that Paul makes in Romans 3:21–31: justification comes through faith; the Gentiles are being brought into the kingdom; creation has been subjected to "frustration"; the invisible attributes of God are clearly seen in nature; there is no one righteous on the earth; creation groans as in childbirth

- In Romans 4:13 we find a universalizing of the land promise, the promise of many descendants, the promise that Abraham would be the means of blessing "all the peoples of the earth," and that the promise is not received through the Law.

- It is probable that Paul, in Ephesians 6:2–3, understands the promise accompanying the commandment about obedient children to involve living for a long time on the earth in a physical sense.

- New creation: the new world of re-creation that God has made to dawn in Christ and in which everyone who is in Christ is included

Reflection Questions

1. Is the New Testament unconcerned with the natural world? Has it contributed to the neglect of the environment in our day? Explain.

2. What role does the land play in the development of God's redemptive plan in the Old Testament? Does the Old Testament end with these promises fulfilled? How does the "land" become the "world" in Romans?

3. Describe the use of "new creation" in Galatians 6:15 and 2 Corinthians 5:17.

Discussion Question

1. What are your thoughts on the debate concerning how the Old Testament land promise will be fulfilled in "the last days"? Will it be purely spiritual or physical? What does this mean for creation care?

Quiz

1. Which apostle quotes Joel 2:28–32 in his sermon in Acts 2?

    a) John
    b) Peter
    c) Paul
    d) James

2. (T/F) New Testament soteriology falls into an "already/not yet" pattern.

3. Interest in the world of creation is evident in which group of biblical books?

    a) The Gospels
    b) The Pauline Epistles
    c) The General Epistles
    d) The apocalyptic literature

4. (T/F) The letters of the New Testament say little about the world of nature.

5. Land was one of the basic components of God's original promise to whom?

   a) Noah
   b) Jacob
   c) Abraham
   d) Isaac

6. Jesus and the apostles suggest that the land promise has been ____.

   a) Particularized
   b) Universalized
   c) Personalized
   d) Specialized

7. Where does Paul promise children that if they obey their parents it will go "well" with them and they will "enjoy long life on the earth"?

   a) Ephesians 6:2–3
   b) Ephesians 5:22–33
   c) Ephesians 6:5–9
   d) Ephesians 5:15–20

8. Which is NOT one of the Jewish texts outside of the New Testament that contains the phrase "new creation"?

   a) 1 Maccabees
   b) Jubilees
   c) 1 Enoch
   d) The Dead Sea Scroll of the "Hymns"

9. (T/F) In the texts where Paul uses the phrase "new creation," he applies the language to the current situation of Christian believers.

10. The cosmic scope of God's redemptive work in Christ is made even more clear in which text?

   a) 2 Corinthians 5:17
   b) Galatians 3:28
   c) Ephesians 6:2–3
   d) Colossians 1:20

ANSWER KEY
1. B, 2. F, 3. A, 4. T, 5. C, 6. B, 7. A, 8. A, 9. T, 10. D

CHAPTER 9

"I Am Making Everything New!"

You Should Know

- Transformation model: Creation, though changed in certain ways, will endure into eternity.
- Romans 8:19–22 is the most important passage in the New Testament about the future of creation. In it we find that creation is said to "groan," believers should be patient in times of suffering, Christians' glorification means the liberation of creation, and Paul is talking about *ktisis*.
- *Ktisis*: "creation"
- *Heurethēsetai*: "will be found"
- About the future creation, Romans 8:19–22 makes the point that creation has a future and God will transform creation.
- Green utopianism: an idea popular with environmentalists that if our own programs are fully implemented they will usher in environmental nirvana
- Second Peter 3:3–14 parallels the flood narrative, suggesting that God will "destroy" this world by judging evil and transforming creation.
- The Greek word for "new" that John uses in Revelation 21:1 generally connotes a renewal of what already exists.

Reflection Questions

1. Describe the various models for creation's end. Which is the best and why?

2. Summarize the "two vital points" Romans 8:19–22 makes about what the future of creation will look like. Why must Christians resist "green utopianism"?

3. Summarize the different translations for the end of 2 Peter 3:10. Which one has nearly all recent commentators and English translations adopted?

Discussion Question

1. How does the New Testament suggest we should read Old Testament promises about Israel's land? What implications would this reading have for our understanding of the flow of biblical teaching and the present state of creation?

Quiz

1. Which is the most important passage in the New Testament about the future of creation?

   a) Romans 8:19–22
   b) Romans 4:13
   c) Romans 1:18–21
   d) Romans 3:21–26

2. Which is NOT one of the things Romans 8:19–22 teaches about the future of creation?

   a) Creation's "frustration" will likely be removed in the future
   b) Creation will be liberated from its bondage to decay
   c) Creation will be brought into the freedom and glory of the children of God
   d) Creation will be remade as Christ ushers in the new heavens and new earth

3. Romans 8 teaches what view of creation?

   a) Replacement
   b) Transformation

    c) Purely spiritual existence in heaven

    d) Utopian

4. (T/F) Second Peter 3:3–14 teaches a "replacement" model of creation's end.

5. (T/F) Nearly all recent commentators and English translations translate the end of 2 Peter 3:10 as "will be found."

6. In the Old Testament, what often connotes God's judgment?

    a) Fire

    b) Wind

    c) Clouds

    d) Floods

7. The natural world has a larger place in _____ than in any other New Testament book.

    a) 2 Peter

    b) Romans

    c) Colossians

    d) Revelation

8. (T/F) According to 1 Corinthians 15:51, our bodies will be replaced, not changed.

9. If then, "everything is going to burn," the fire must be a _____ fire.

    a) Destroying

    b) Refining

    c) Replacing

    d) Spiritual

10. (T/F) The biblical view of human beings is that embodiment is a fundamental aspect of who we are as persons.

ANSWER KEY

1. A, 2. D, 3. B, 4. F, 5. T, 6. A, 7. D, 8. F, 9. B, 10. T

CHAPTER 10

The Gospel and Creation Care

You Should Know

- Romans 12:2 says that Christians are transformed when their minds are renewed.

- Creation care is part of the gospel itself.

- Creation care can never be separated for Christians from the transformation of people that is central to the gospel.

- The phrase "good news" is about the Son of God, mediates salvation, is the eschatological Jubilee, and is about the inaugurated kingdom of Jesus Christ.

- *Basar*: "announce news"

- The New Testament writers were especially influenced by the "good news" language in the prophetic book of Isaiah.

- Good news: In the Old Testament, this phrase refers broadly to God's promise to exert his kingly power on behalf of his oppressed people.

- Important consequences for creation care we can draw from the gospel: There is no conflict between gospel and creation care; the gospel is designed to transform our thinking about the world.

- Alister McGrath agrees that "human self-centeredness is the root of our ecological crisis," but argues that "the most self-centered religion in history is the secular creed of twentieth-century Western culture, whose roots lie in the Enlightenment of the eighteenth century and whose foundation belief is that humanity is the arbiter of all ideas and values."

Reflection Questions

1. Are evangelism and creation care at odds with one another? Explain. How does creation care relate to the "good news"?

2. Summarize the Old Testament's use of "good news" language. In what ways did the Old Testament "good news" passages influence the New Testament writers?

3. Explain both the first important consequence and second important consequence for creation care from this unit's discussion of gospel.

Discussion Question

1. In your own words, summarize this session's focus on the relationship between creation care and the gospel. Provide a biblical-theological treatment of "good news" language throughout the Bible.

Quiz

1. Which verse describes the transformation of Christians whose minds are being renewed?

    a) Romans 12:2
    b) 1 Corinthians 15:44
    c) 1 Corinthians 1:23
    d) Romans 10:14

2. (T/F) One of the reasons many Christians are not motivated to take care of God's creation is ignorance.

3. (T/F) Becoming involved in genuine creation care can be a time-consuming endeavor.

4. To be human means to _____ the earth for God's glory.

    a) Guard and preserve
    b) Cultivate and watch
    c) Till and observe
    d) Work and keep

5. Which verse says, "How can they hear without someone preaching to them?"

    a) Romans 12:2

    b) 1 Corinthians 15:44

    c) Romans 10:14

    d) 1 Corinthians 1:23

6. (T/F) The "good news" is focused on the kingdom that is inaugurated in the first coming of Jesus.

7. Where does Paul say to live "in a manner worthy of the gospel of Christ"? (174)

    a) Romans 1:2–4

    b) Philippians 1:27

    c) Colossians 1:10

    d) Galatians 1:7

8. (T/F) "Good news" language is found in both Isaiah 40:9 and Isaiah 52:7.

9. Where does Jesus summarize his ministry by incorporating the "good news" language from Isaiah 61:1?

    a) Luke 4:18

    b) Matthew 4:23

    c) Matthew 9:35

    d) Luke 16:16

10. Which are the important consequences for creation care derived from this discussion of gospel?

    a) There is no conflict between gospel and creation care

    b) The gospel is designed to transform how we think about the world

    c) Evangelism takes precedence over creation care

    d) All of the above

    e) Both A & B

CHAPTER 11

Humans and Creation: Understanding Our Place

You Should Know

- Speciesism: The human species is superior to all others.

- The central tenet of modern ecological science is the realization that everything is connected.

- Ruling is qualified by serving.

- Creation ethics: The way the universe is determines how man ought to behave himself in it.

- Any antithesis between creation and "other regard" is at bottom quite artificial because God often asks us to do more than one thing; creation care and "other regard" go hand-in-hand.

- The accountability side of the stewardship metaphor means that as stewards of creation, human beings must please creation's owner, the Lord God.

Reflection Questions

1. In what ways are humans central players in the biblical drama of creation and redemption?

2. If the question is not whether humans will "rule" the earth, then what is it? Discuss sin's role in this.

3. How do the two "great commandments" relate to creation care? What does "other regard" mean?

Discussion Question

1. Summarize humans' place in creation.

Quiz

1. (T/F) Only humans were made "in God's image."

2. Which part(s) make(s) up our focus about the place of humans in "creation care"?

    a) Active
    b) Passive
    c) Receptive
    d) Both A & B
    e) Both A & C

3. What is the label some environmentalists apply to the view that sees human species as superior to all others?

    a) Speciesism
    b) Humanism
    c) Absolutism
    d) Human totalitarianism

4. (T/F) The central tenet of modern ecological science is the realization that everything is connected.

5. What the _____ bent into a focus on the self, the second Adam turns back into a focus on God.

    a) Fall
    b) Woman
    c) First Adam
    d) Serpent

6. (T/F) A popular way of capturing the vital balance between "ruling" and "serving" is the language of regency.

7. Human "rule over creation" is seriously conditioned by the _____ focus of Genesis 1 and of the entire scriptural account.

a) Anthropocentric
b) Soteriocentric
c) Hamartiocentric
d) Theocentric

8. Which passage says, "Each of you should use whatever gift you have received to serve others, as faithful stewards of God's grace in its various forms"?

a) 1 Corinthians 4:1–2
b) 1 Peter 4:10
c) Titus 1:7
d) Luke 16:1–8

9. Who espouses "creation ethics"?

a) Oliver O'Donovan
b) Alister McGrath
c) Philip Hughes
d) Colin Gunton

10. (T/F) Some contemporary scholars are using the language of "other regard" to capture the command to love our neighbors.

CHAPTER 12

Wisdom and Creation Care

You Should Know

- The theology of creation provides few specific and practical guidelines for responsible Christian decision-making.

- Thomas Derr and Arne Naess are theologians who are pessimistic about the practical usefulness of a theology of creation.

- Key takeaways from the discussion about the Keystone XL: Some favor economics over environment; some focus on the politics; some focus on environmental implications; people holding the same basic theology about creation come to different conclusions.

- 1 Corinthians 4:2: Paul says that a steward is to be "faithful."

- What Scripture tells us about the nature of our world: Creation is fashioned for us to inhabit; creation is designed to stimulate worship of God; we must steward with care; God intends creation to last forever.

- Three aspects of wisdom that will help guide us to faithful stewardship of creation: 1) learning about our world, 2) making good decisions, and 3) appreciating our limitations

- A wise person is one who governs his or her life in accordance with the reality of the world as God has made it.

- Proverbs 16:1: "To humans belong the plans of the heart, but from the Lord comes the proper answer of the tongue."

- Both conservation and development are integral aspects of human rule of the earth.

Reflection Questions

1. Why is Thomas Derr pessimistic about the practical usefulness of a theology of creation? Are the reservations of Derr and Naess justified? Explain.

2. Summarize the Keystone XL case study. What is the overall point?

3. How should the Christian who wants to be a "faithful" steward of creation relate to science? Do you agree or disagree? Why?

Discussion Question

1. Summarize the relationship of wisdom and creation care. Do you agree that this is what "stewardship" should look like?

Quiz

1. (T/F) The theology of creation that has emerged from our survey of the story of creation in Scripture has been theoretical.

2. Who argues that Scripture does not reveal enough about God's intentions for nature to enable us to make reasoned ethical decisions?

    a) Arne Naess
    b) Thomas Derr
    c) Eberhard Jüngel
    d) Christoph Schwöbel

3. Who objects to the "stewardship" metaphor as a way of characterizing the relation of humans and nature?

    a) Thomas Derr
    b) Arne Naess
    c) Eberhard Jüngel
    d) Christof Schwöbel

4. Paul says in 1 Corinthians 4:2 that a steward is to be which of the following?

    a) Brave
    b) True

    c) Faithful

    d) Meek

5. (T/F) The Christian who wants to be a "faithful" steward of creation will shun scientific data.

6. Who said, "If the world the Christian message talks about is the same as the world investigated by the sciences, we have to assume that the findings of the sciences have some connection to what Christians believe the world to be"?

    a) Eberhard Jüngel

    b) Thomas Derr

    c) Arne Naess

    d) Christof Schwöbel

7. (T/F) The vast majority of scientists working in this field agree in significant ways about climate change, its causes, and its consequences.

8. Which is NOT one of the aspects of wisdom that will help Christians steward faithfully?

    a) Learning about our world

    b) Making good decisions

    c) Dialoguing with environmentalists

    d) Appreciating our limitations

9. Biblical wisdom involves _____, from a divine perspective, on the realities of the created world.

    a) Careful planning

    b) Reflection

    c) Stewardship

    d) Fear of the LORD

10. Who said, "What we need is a form of control which is capable of controlling itself"?

    a) Eberhard Jüngel

    b) Christof Schwöbel

    c) Arne Naess

    d) Thomas Derr

ANSWER KEY

1. T, 2. B, 3. B, 4. C, 5. F, 6. D, 7. T, 8. C, 9. B, 10. A

CHAPTER 13

Creation in Crisis?

You Should Know

- Two things missing from our educational system most necessary for cultivating the knowledge and wisdom we need concerning creation care: focused attention to the particularities of a place and its life; attention to complex global challenges

- The rule of humankind as described in Genesis 1:28 is, strictly speaking, not over the earth itself but over other creatures.

- Natural or background rate of biodiversity loss: Over time some species, due to competition or a changing environment, fail to reproduce at greater rates than they die.

- The estimated decrease, between 1970 and 2010, in the total number of wild mammals, birds, reptiles, amphibians, and fish around the globe according to the Living Planet Report: 52%

- The primary driver of the decline in the diversity and abundance of other life on earth is the loss of suitable habitat in which other creatures can live.

- Anthropocene: the term that describes humankind's influence exerted on the planet, comparable to a major geological force

- Deforestation is the most obvious and well-known global example of our collective negative effect on earth, caused by fuel, building materials, consumption habits, and agriculture.

- Solutions to the overuse and misapplication of nitrogen and phosphorous fertilizers: crop rotation, new crop varieties, recycling nutrients, greater carefulness in applying fertilizer

Reflection Questions

1. In what ways does our contemporary culture make it dangerously easy for most people to remain ignorant about the status and functioning of the very things that sustain life?

2. What is by far the primary driver of the decline in the diversity and abundance of other life on earth? Explain humankind's ever-expanding influence on the earth.

3. What is the difference between the warming that attended our emergence from the most recent ice age and the warming that we are experiencing today? What is the cause of our recent global warming?

Discussion Question

1. Make a list of some ideas for how our Christian faith might shape the way we care for creation and live in relationship to others and the earth in our time and place.

Quiz

1. (T/F) The rule of humankind as described in Genesis 1 is not over other creatures but over the earth itself.

2. There is what scientists call a _____ rate of biodiversity loss, as over time some species, due to competition or a changing environment, fail to reproduce at greater rates than they die.

    a) "Benign" or "inconsequential"
    b) "Natural" or "background"
    c) "Malignant" or "malicious"
    d) "Rapid" or "extreme"

3. Humankind now exerts an influence on our planet that is comparable to a major geological force, leading some to dub our age _____.

    a) Priene
    b) Nicene
    c) Anthropocene
    d) Theocene

4. (T/F) An estimated eighty-three percent of the earth's ice-free land is now directly influenced by human beings in one way or another.

5. Which is NOT a cause of deforestation?

    a) Wildfires

    b) Fuel

    c) Building materials

    d) Small-scale subsistence farming

6. Oceanic and freshwater dead zones are one of the unfortunate consequences of agriculture's reliance on which of the following?

    a) Deforestation

    b) Oil

    c) Synthetic fertilizers

    d) Hydroponic fisheries

7. (T/F) Widespread use of synthetic fertilizer is contributing to the degradation and loss of our topsoil.

8. According to the deputy director of the UN's Food and Agriculture Organization, at the current rate of topsoil loss and degradation, the world's soils may be able to support how many years of harvests?

    a) Fifty

    b) Seventy

    c) Forty

    d) Sixty

9. What are the two key differences between the warming that attended our emergence from the most recent ice age and the warming that we are experiencing today?

    a) The cause of the recent warming and the planet's current rate of warming

    b) The amount of time that has elapsed and the cause of the recent warming

    c) The last warming was compensatory and the scarcity of the planet's current plants and animals

    d) The cause of the recent warming and the scarcity of the planet's current plants and animals

10. What is the name of the group of scientists who have attempted to determine boundaries within which human activity must be constrained if the earth is to be able to go on supporting human life?

    a) Planetary boundaries
    b) Earthly boundaries
    c) Milk Way boundaries
    d) Universal boundaries

CHAPTER 14

Caring for Creation and Worshipping the Creator

You Should Know

- First necessary practice: teach and preach the whole gospel

- Secondary necessary practice: a posture towards God's creation of gratefulness, joy, and worship

- Pastors' main priorities are always preaching the Word and administering the Sacraments. Therefore, laypeople will need to organize and do much of the on-the-ground work in creation care.

- An ignorance of the earth's history obscures the reality that our time is unique in many respects.

- Paul, in 1 Thessalonians 5:6, calls for us metaphorically to "be awake and sober."

- The acronym "AWAKE": attentiveness, walking, activism, konsumerism, eating

- Legitimate forms of activism: protesting, voting, signing petitions, supporting the church

- The most important and radical thing we can do personally to care better for creation is to stop.

Reflection Questions

1. Describe the first necessary practice.

2. Describe the second necessary practice.

3. Why is activism important? Where is the best place to start with our activism?

Discussion Question

1. Looking back at everything you've learned, have your views on creation and Christians' role within it changed? In your opinion, what is the role of creation in God's story of redemption?

Quiz

1. (T/F) Caring for creation is to see our keeping of the earth as extricable from the gospel itself.

2. What is the first necessary practice for us all, especially those in leadership?

    a) Lobby for better environmental plans that reflect creation care values

    b) Teach and preach the whole gospel

    c) Teach better agricultural practices

    d) Be more mindful of what and how much we consume

3. (T/F) Paul preached the gospel for the first time to those who had no background knowledge of the Old Testament as recorded in Acts 12 and 15.

4. What is the second necessary practice for us all?

    a) Teach and preach the whole gospel

    b) Be more mindful of what and how much we consume

    c) Lobby for better environmental plans that reflect creation care values

    d) A posture towards God's creation of gratefulness, joy, and worship

5. If we are to be awakened to the beauty and goodness of non-human creation around us, we must make time in our lives to do what?

    a) Take a nature class

    b) Learn good environmental practices

    c) Disengage from our technological culture

    d) Be more mindful of what and how much we consume

6. (T/F) Usually, to claim that your own time is unique betrays an ignorance of history.

7. Who said, "The right thing to do today, as always, is to stop, or start stopping, our habit of wasting and poisoning the good and beautiful things of the world, which once were called 'divine gifts' and now are called 'natural resources'"?

    a) Wendell Berry

    b) Walter Brueggemann

    c) Henry David Thoreau

    d) Aldo Leopold

8. Who said, "To be awake is to be alive"?

    a) Wendell Berry

    b) Walter Brueggemann

    c) Aldo Leopold

    d) Henry David Thoreau

9. What is perhaps the best way to connect or reconnect with our local community?

    a) Driving a car

    b) Walking

    c) Flying in a plane

    d) Jogging

10. All of us need to become _____ at some level if we are to take seriously both the demands of the gospel and the realities of our current situation.

    a) Activists

    b) Environmentalists

    c) Lobbyists

    d) Scientists

ANSWER KEY

1. F, 2. B, 3. F, 4. D, 5. C, 6. T, 7. A, 8. D, 9. B, 10. A

Notes